DS
135
.F9
D86

Duncan, David
Douglas.

The fragile miracle
of Martin Gray

DATE			
OCT 9 '86			

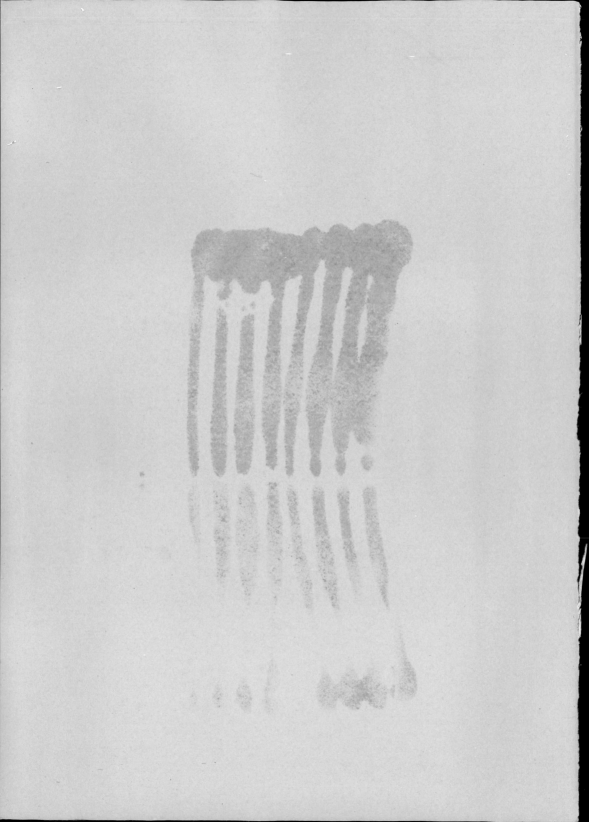

the fragile miracle
of
martin gray

the fragile miracle
of
martin gray

PHOTOGRAPHS AND TEXT
BY
david douglas duncan

ABBEVILLE PRESS, INC. • PUBLISHERS
NEW YORK, N.Y.

photography and text
DAVID DOUGLAS DUNCAN

photographic masterprints
DAN BECKER—NEW YORK
CARMINE ERCOLANO—LIFE

preface one and two
Martin Gray's snapshot albums
Anonymous WW II photographers
pages 32–33—PIERRE DOMENECH

printing and binding
DAI NIPPON—TOKYO, JAPAN

copyright © 1979 by Cross River Press, Ltd.
Library of Congress 79-88970
ISBN 0-89659-073-9

Books by D. D. D.

The Fragile Miracle of Martin Gray
Magic Worlds of Fantasy
The Silent Studio
Goodbye Picasso
Prismatics
War Without Heroes
Self-Portrait: USA
I Protest!
Yankee Nomad
Picasso's Picassos
Treasures of The Kremlin
The Private World of Pablo Picasso
This Is War!

DEDICATED TO MARTIN

AND HIS LOST CHILDHOOD

There are no scales for weighing sadness, no vessels for measuring fallen tears. When facing others' sorrows, one rarely soothes the agony and almost never finds a road to the heart. Understatement or exaggeration often result from searching for words to ease the grief of a friend. That also was a hazard in now telling this story of a man who is worth remembering.

D. D. D.

contents

foreword

Once upon a time, there was a half-blind man who invented the miracle that transformed his tormented life. His religion was faith in oneself, love of the earth, and trust in other men—even though the ultimate violences of man and nature had twice destroyed everyone *he* loved.

*   *   *   *   *

Martin Gray was born part Catholic and part Jewish on the prosperous side of the Warsaw ghetto, fourteen years before Hitler began World War II by attacking Poland. By the time the war ended, all the members of his family, except for an uncle and grandmother in New York, had died in the fighting or in concentration camp gas chambers. He fought as a child street guerrilla against the Nazis in Warsaw, was confined in Treblinka, escaped, joined the Polish partisans in the forests and then the Russian army. He celebrated his nineteenth birthday while attacking Berlin. Later, he made his way into the American lines to become a counterespionage agent, tracking Martin Bormann through the villages of Bavaria; he then sailed for the United States as a penniless émigré. After making a fortune importing truckloads of Bavarian porcelain, he married a ravishingly beautiful Dutch girl with whom he moved to the south of France, where they were raising a family of two sons and two daughters when a forest fire swept around their remote hilltop. All but Martin perished. It was October 3, 1970.

The day after the fire, southern France was blanketed in fog and lashed by unending rainstorms, both probably caused by countless tons of wood ash hurled into the Mediterranean skies—rain that came too late. Martin still numbly searched his empty paradise for his family, a combat casualty without visible wounds—a familiar sight on any battlefield. He had, however, burned his shoulder and feet while helping a smoke-blinded neighbor escape from another hillock, after assuming that his own family had driven safely to the nearby seashore. But they never arrived; and they would have been unharmed had they only stayed within the ancient stone walls of their home and not fled, for the fire leapfrogged the vine-festooned house, with its cork oaks and cypress trees and ornamental plume grass-fringed garden, leaving everything unscathed.

Martin and Dina and their children were my neighbors. Two pictures I took of Martin after the fire were printed in the French magazine *Paris-Match*, together with the story of his double tragedy; at Treblinka and at Tanneron, his devastated Mediterranean hilltop. Several publishers saw the article and persuaded Martin to reveal the ordeals of his life in a book, which has now been translated into eighteen languages and aroused a reader response of flood proportions. Martin has answered every letter. All royalties from his book have been donated to a fund that sponsors campaigns for children's fire protection education, supports reforestation programs in France, and contributes to the purchase of firefighting equipment used along the Mediterranean. Martin has now also written several more books, inspired by the letters from those who have been scarred by life, though none so deeply as himself.

Martin rarely talked about himself before the fire. Never a word revealing where he came from, or details about his family, or how he had broken his nose or been blinded in his left eye (hand-to-hand fighting with a German soldier during the fall of Warsaw). For some reason—perhaps it was his accent—I always assumed he was born in Russia. But then there were vague references to Berlin and Polish partisans and counterespionage and the American army. Even when I headed for assignments with the Marines in Vietnam and drove up to his falcon's nest of a home on its windswept hilltop to say goodbye, Martin never revealed the slightest familiarity with war or fightingmen. As always, he was an exuberant mystery. He and Dina waved good-luck, their arms filled with squirming, waving children, flanked by two of the most terrifying guard dogs that money and training could provide. Martin protected his family when away from home. A treasure of a family on a radiant hilltop. I looked at all of those joyous faces and, as happens so often, took them for granted. I never photographed them—not once.

One of the giant dogs died with Dina and the children in the car when they tried to outrun the flames. His mate, Lady, stayed behind with Martin at the house and survived. She was broken by the fire, never again to bark, challenge strangers, or even look one in the eye. Three weeks after the catastrophe she disappeared alone across the charred horizon to die.

My wife Sheila and I first met Martin and Dina one afternoon sixteen or seventeen years ago—anyway, Nicole was only an infant and the other children hadn't yet arrived, so it must have been eighteen years ago. We were exploring the untrampled, mimosa-mantled ridgeline of Tanneron, a few miles west of our home on the southern coast of France near Grasse. Eighteen years ago, Tanneron was just another obscure, bypassed hilltown on the Riviera—and it still is: a village of strawberry farmers, wild boar hunters, two schoolteachers—and the Martin Grays, who lived in a three hundred-year-old fortress of a farmhouse in the saddle of the ridge just south of town.

When Sheila and I first met them, they were camping in two rooms. The rest of the place was a shambles of fallen tiles, dusty cobwebs, timbers that might have been used when building the Great Pyramid of Giza, and murky attics lighted only by the cracks in the roof . . . a place where one might be crippled forever by falling through a floor or two. A marvelous place. It was easy to share Dina's love for it, and their excitement when she shoved aside ink drawings of elaborate delicacy (ballet costumes for Nicole) for others of sweeping simplicity —her dreams of what that old house would eventually become. Martin's finger always poked at the drawings and always stopped just a millimeter short of smudging them. A man of concealed precision. Without a doctor, he delivered three of their four children in that centuries-weathered farmhouse . . . "I wanted to *feel* their lives in those first moments of existence."

It was only after the fire that Martin began to talk about himself. The dam holding back a thousand unbearable lifetimes finally broke. Cataracts of words swept away those barricades guarding his wartime memories and produced his searing book, *For Those I Loved*, which created an almost evangelical life for him among the world of the wounded.

Martin has now remarried. He and his wife Virginia, and their infant daughters Barbara and Larissa, are bringing new life and laughter to that farmhouse on the ridgeline at Tanneron.

He is beginning again.

And today, Martin's message is helping to transform personal disasters into sources of nourishment for resurrecting even the most shattered lives—including his own.

D. D. D.

Castellaras,
France

Warsaw —Treblinka

Almost nothing remains of Martin's childhood. Only a few
self-conscious, cracked and fading studio portraits were saved
by a grandmother in America: one tiny image of his mother;
another of himself, prophetically clutching a toy rifle; several of
his somberly posing little brothers. No picture exists of his father
—his mentor and saint. Even the memories of those first secure
fourteen years with his parents and two younger brothers have
now mostly disappeared, lost in the same carnage that levelled
Warsaw and the ghetto, when Hitler's wrath focused first on
Poland and her Jews. The city has now arisen from its ruins;
so has his life—twice, each time not like before.

6000000 + 3

History books of later years would sum it all up in round figures, with the total an even 6000000—not one more, or less. Six. Easy to remember. Nobody seems to know how many gypsies and "others" were murdered on command, and by the trainload, like Warsaw's Jews—even some with good Catholic ancestors—such as Martin's mother and his two little brothers; and their nanny, and all of their friends and neighbors. In a place at the end of the line, with perhaps the loveliest, most musical name in Poland: Treblinka. Which added to its horror—and from which Martin escaped. His father was shot in the street near their home.

20

Holocaust

Hero
in
Red Army

Orphaned by the gas chambers and a sniper's bullet, Martin returned to Warsaw as a street guerrilla after escaping from Treblinka. The ghetto destroyed, he joined Polish partisans

in the forests, then the Russian army, where he won the highest combat decorations (the Orders of Red Star, Patriotic War, and Alexandre Nevski) and field promotions to captain while fighting across eastern Europe, which ended in the capture of Berlin on his nineteenth birthday. Disenchanted with Soviet agents hiding among the military, he crossed into the American lines, where he became a volunteer counterespionage agent tracking down fleeing Nazis. Turning to New York to find his grandmother, he became a U.S. citizen, earning a fringe living as a tie salesman and a summer resort hotel busboy-waiter-entertainer—and then a fortune in real estate and imported antiques. He also fasted, on water, for thirty-eight days, trying to save his failing good eye; his left one was blinded earlier by a German rifle butt.

Hope
in
America

Martin had landed in New York, after the war, as a destitute, almost classical, refugee who was determined to create not only a new life, but to conquer the New World—fast! Within ten years much of that vision was a reality. His first nickel-pinching investments had become winners, as he tirelessly returned to Europe buying porcelain and antiques, riding the new, booming American market to its crest. Then he parlayed those profits into another bonanza in Canadian real estate, as it skyrocketed, too. Martin became a millionaire. And he found Dina. On first meeting, she told him, "I'd love to have my children with a man like you." Nicole arrived the next year; their honeymoon had been the ride from City Hall back to his shop. Warsaw and Treblinka faded. His dream was complete. Almost! He was again going blind, and had been told time was short. He sold out. Then he took Dina and Nicole, and his willpower, aboard the *Queen Mary*—first class—sailing for France and Mediterranean sunshine, to start whatever still remained of his life, again. They found their paradise in an isolated derelict farmhouse, which they rebuilt, together with their lives.

preface two

Laughter — Silence

Their dream house was a ruin when they found it, but with vast walls that had stood for three full centuries. Love changed them again into a home. Dina and Martin moved to Tanneron with eyes lifted to the stars, and hearts embracing the earth—and the tomorrows of their ever more numerous children. He delivered Dina's three pioneer babies—just as he restored the farmhouse, worked its fields, and looked at his wife—thanking each minute for their, and his, new lives.

Nicole, Suzanne, Richard and Charles; Hercules, Amber and Lady: Martin's family at Tanneron bore slight resemblance to his Warsaw memories, nor were any wounds from Treblinka revealed. At the nearby Cannes Film Festival, where Dina outshone many stars, only she knew Martin's chilling life's story, rougher than any movie script. Their skyline farmhouse was within minutes of legendary casinos gilding the French Riviera, yet they sought simple lives in a world apart.

Children and love ruled the hilltop.
If Martin left it even for a moment,
laughter, waving arms, blown kisses
and sweeping curtsies followed him.
And voices calling "Goodbye Daddy!"

ruins

No rain had fallen for months. It was a classic year for wine connoisseurs. Each morning gnarled faces turned to the haze-filtered autumn sky, silently praying. The annual *vendange*, grape harvest, would soon begin among the sprawling French vineyards. With the promise of regal vintages only a few weeks away, rain now could easily sabotage the year's work, leaving little more than sheds filled with moisture-sodden grapes, suitable only for ordinary bistro wine or as fruit for the table. In every farmhouse, every village, every château, the prayer was the same: *"Please . . . no rain!"*

The mistral came instead—wind that dominates all life in the
wine country of southern France . . . an ever-stronger west wind
that howls for days: three, six, nine—wind that bends the
trunks of great black oaks and slender river cypresses alike,
canting them and the groves of ancient olives, hedgerows,
and all the flowers to the east . . . an endless gale that quickly
dehydrates men and foliage, sapping life's juices even in the
deepest forests, leaving shaded ferns brittle and the earth itself
parched—defenseless.

After the fire, a voiceless sadness lay upon the blackened
hilltops surrounding Tanneron, and Martin learned the truth of
his being again alone. Dina and the children and their enormous
guard dog had never reached the coast but were caught by their
eternity, racing toward them behind suffocating smoke.
The firestorm had burst through the treetops, probed into every
protective ravine and then cut the escape road to the sea.
High-tension wires on the cross-country power pylons west of
Tanneron had probably swayed wildly—and touched—during
the worst of the mistral, when its velocity was over a hundred
miles an hour, cascading showers of sparks down upon the
reeling, gunpowder-dry trees.

The mistral faded and died at dusk of the first night. Dina and
the children were gone. Shouts imploring them to run echoed
through the empty house. Martin was reliving his Warsaw
nightmare, feeling its flames again reaching for him from the
nearby forest. Then, cloudburst followed cloudburst to soothe
all wounds and rinse the ashes from that tortured land.

35

Martin roamed the hilltop
waiting for his wife who
would never return . . .
and he listened for his
children racing home from
their two-room school,
down the narrow road,
in Tanneron village.

And for the laughter
—now silent forever.

In the wake of every war, corrosive images survive of refugees clamoring for food and mercy, of fire-blackened homes abandoned to looters, of columns of prisoners already faceless in sullen surrender, of pristine fields sown with grotesque machines and crumpled bodies, brothers of those other men who fell in the rubble of cities under siege.

Wars within a man's head can be equally as cruel, with no one aware of them—without leaving a mark.

*　*　*　*　*

Martin stood motionless at his door not feeling the rain, as a flood of lost faces from Warsaw and Treblinka, and now Tanneron, threatened to destroy him and all remnants of his tragic life. Offers of help never reached him. Distant voices of those he loved already had deafened him to others trying to comfort him after the fire.

An old shepherd's cape protected the shoulder he burned while rescuing a bedridden peasant neighbor from a shack on the nearest hill, when he thought his own family was safe. Ironically, his wife, four children, and their killer guard dog never escaped. Her car had plunged over an embankment in the smoke and they were trapped, less than a mile from home. With only their bodies, Dina and that heroic dog had attempted to shield the children during those frantic final moments before the inferno torched the trees above them while searching for their hiding place.

Lady wilted when her mate perished with Dina. She never barked again, never raised her head, never ate again. Three weeks after the fire she vanished into the mists along the horizon to die. Then only Martin heard voices at Tanneron.

41

Very little could have been seen on the battlefield at Tanneron,
where the willpower of Martin Gray fought for control of
his emotions and memories, and for domination of his future life.
It was total warfare. No thought was given to surrender.
From a distance, nothing betrayed the raging conflict; his good
right eye measured the enemy, while his left was unfathomable—
blind since earlier hand-to-hand combat at night in the ghetto.

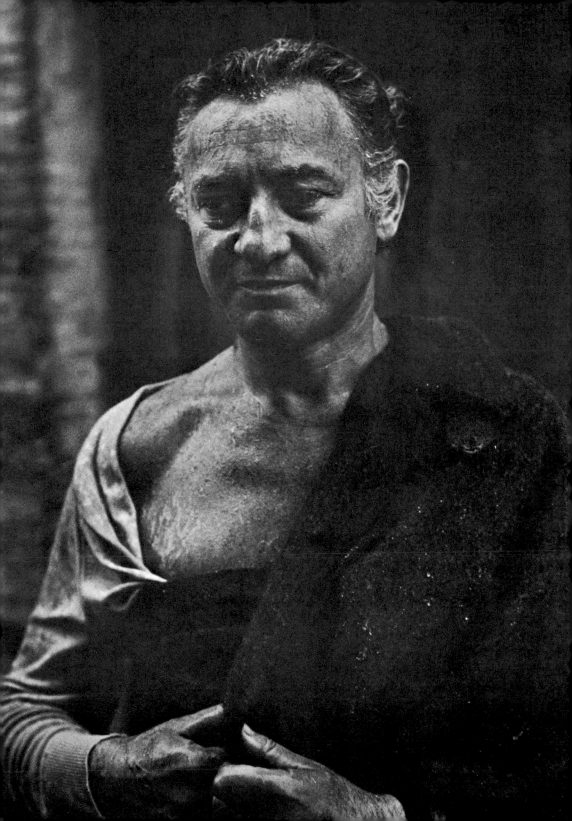

After Dina and the four children died, rain and drear mist enshrouded Tanneron and the hilltop world they left behind. The house was nearly invisible, even from the new garden chairs where all of them had been sitting when Martin first smelled burning leaves. Dragging his chair close to the house, an old lookout post, he had shouted for Dina to herd the children inside as he ran to phone the gendarmes and other fire watchers. Smoke was turning daylight to dusk—and the children panicked.

Recalling earlier terror among the children of Warsaw when fires reduced it to ashes, Martin approved Dina's plan of escaping to a haven only five minutes away down the road to the sea. Both knew the local peasants' code of never leaving the protection of an old stone farmhouse during a forest fire, but there seemed to be plenty of time. Martin stayed behind to spray water on the wooden doors and shutters and on a nearly full furnace oil tank that would blow the roof off if it exploded.

The firestorm incinerated the entire countryside but left the hilltop safe and silent, almost serene, after it had passed. Just as at Treblinka, Martin had survived once more. And as before, in Warsaw and then Treblinka, he would never see any of his family again.

Dina with her sketches, and Martin with a lone Calabrian
master of all trades, had slowly transformed their ruin of a
farmhouse into an enchanted place, so vast that one corner
became a studio where Dina taught the children ballet and
painting and how to design and sew costumes for school parties.
And it was there that they learned the piano and practiced on
their accordions, when not listening to classical music and to
voices recorded long before they were born.

In the oak-beamed living room, Martin read to them and
told stories of pioneers' visions and lands of promise . . .
of their need to discover *their* God and to have faith in men.

But then Dina and Nicole and Suzanne and Charles and baby
Richard and their beloved guard dog died. And Lady would
soon disappear forever into the gloom of a dead forest. And
Martin would again be alone, except for a vacant-eyed kitten,
also staring at nothing across an empty living room.

the fragile miracle

For many nights after the fire, Martin prowled the darkness
of his silent home—a frenzied, stricken creature trapped within
those ancient walls, trying to escape from himself. He began
reliving the agonies of Warsaw and Treblinka, seeing again the
closeup face of war. He called out to other lost children who had
perished years before in the ghetto, where his own childhood
had died. He asked for no mercy from his haunting memories—
but he would never again remain mute about the past.

During the first several years after his book appeared, Martin
crisscrossed western Europe to speak—always without fees—
before audiences of students and civic groups, coal miners
and factory workers, parliamentary committees, prime ministers,
a reigning king, religious congregations, disabled war veterans,
and on the radio and national television programs. Fluent in six
languages, he spoke first about children: save the children . . .
from war, from fire, from ignorance of the real world surrounding
them. Then he spoke of optimism and of having no fear of fate,
and of his constant search for hope in the debris of disasters:
"One can *always* rebuild, even from ruins!" His faith in willpower
was nearly a religion, with himself its most persuasive disciple.

"Look!"—his life story seemed almost to shout—"It works!"

now each season
will live again

A man must create the world
of which he is the center.

This can be a masterwork:
the painting of an artist,
the piece of a cabinetmaker,
the field of a peasant,
the symphony of a composer,
the page of a writer.

It can be a family.

And when tragedy comes,
as it will, we must take this
suffering into our hands
and, through willpower,
transform it into a fruit
that will nourish us
as we begin life again.

This is the fragile miracle
hidden within us all.

Even after the tragedies at Treblinka and Tanneron, Martin
never lost confidence in other men, or his love for the ravaged
hilltops around his now empty home. And it was there, in the
depths of anguish, that he found within himself the words with
which to answer his question of why he should face life again.

62

In the first years after the Tanneron fire and the loss of his second family, Martin depended solely upon himself, his faith—his willpower, a private god—while he fought to shape his own destiny, instead of just quitting. After his book, *For Those I Loved*, was published and his story widely known, after his name became a pivot of controversy in dinner table discussions when the subjects of survival and Fate and God arose, he still revealed absolutely nothing even when more disasters befell him. He always fought his battles alone.

The letter arrived by hand, without stamps, from the village post office, which also served as the office of the mayor of Tanneron. It was a personal invitation from the Prime Minister of the Republic, who hoped that Monsieur Martin Gray might find the time to call upon him when next in Paris.

Martin was already scheduled to meet a specialist who had been trying to save his failing right eye, injured when he lost his other while fighting in the streets of Warsaw, where his father was shot. Due to malnutrition, he had become semi-blind before escaping the gas chambers of Treblinka, where his mother and the rest of his family died.

The Prime Minister waited to receive him but Martin never appeared. He had been struck from behind on his blind side by a speeding car while crossing the street to the Prime Minister's residence. The Riviera's local newspaper next morning carried a few lines reporting Martin Gray's being confined to a Paris hospital with a nearly fractured spine. That night, thieves with tow chains drove a truck up to Martin's empty hilltop home, yanked open the doors and shutters, and then ransacked it.

Friends sometimes joked with Martin, telling him that had he been born a bit more Catholic he would have qualified perfectly as a commander of medieval Crusaders carrying his banner into battle to recapture the Holy Land. Actually, he looked more like a Roman legionnaire who might have marched with Caesar. His enthusiasm and sheer animal energy were sometimes overwhelming, almost abrasive. He was a primitive who could be stopped by nothing—the final survivor, whose coat of arms might have been emblazoned with "I Am My Faith." He was irresistible even when submerged in the blackest gloom—which he never revealed. Two years after the fire, he remarried the image in his memory. Bernadette looked like Dina, was as radiantly blonde and nearly as beautiful as Dina, was also Dutch like Dina, tried to be as devoted as Dina, and was sometimes even called Dina—which they both quickly and quietly recognized she was not, and would never be. Then Martin was again alone.

Wild mimosa began to bloom again six years after the fire. Martin was ecstatic: an American wanted to buy the old farmhouse as a hideaway from the outside materialistic world, as a haven in which to raise his family—nine children! This was the scene Martin's imagination always had projected of *his* family on that hilltop. He carefully stored all of his treasured remaining possessions in one room, to be moved when he found another place to live: photographs of his lost families, first copies of various language editions of his book, countless carefully cartoned letters from readers of his story. Then he closed the door and left Tanneron, promising to come again in a few months, when the new owner could pay him. Martin really believed in other men. When he returned and knocked at the door he looked into the muzzle of a rifle held by one of the teenage daughters. Shouts from the living room threatened death if he approached the house again. A task force of gendarmes and customs agents converged on the hilltop at dawn. Martin's isolated home had been used as the assembly yard and resale rendezvous point for dozens of unlicensed and smuggled antique cars.

That "ideal" family had also wreaked more havoc upon the venerable old house in three months than three centuries of exposure to other men and nature. Its great oak beams had been chopped from the ceiling for firewood; sledgehammers had shattered most of the floor tiles; rifle slugs and shotgun pellets were embedded everywhere and had sieved the windows, rustic furniture, light fixtures and the refrigerator; while Dina's newly installed radiators had been uprooted and tossed into the yard, among the stacks of splintered packing crates that had once concealed auto parts and now were strewn with Martin's books, family snapshot albums and his book readers' letters . . . all congealing into a rain-and-mud-cemented, slowly moldering mass. Martin looked down at the chaos, the loved debris of two destroyed lifetimes, and then turned to his home, without a word, to start again.

When Martin and Virginia were married, he brought her to his hilltop, where mimosa and peach trees cloaked the scarred earth that held their roots. The fragrance of lavender would soon fill the air. And it was Virginia who looked across the hilltop at the fortress-farmhouse, then up at her husband, and promised, "Now each season will live again."

The First Cry
of
Life
of
Barbara
the
daughter
of
Virginia and Martin Gray
was heard
February Twenty-sixth
at
Tanneron.
Mother and daughter
are well.
The father
is too happy to speak.
Please
do not respond
but as a sign of friendship
for Barbara
plant a flower or tree.

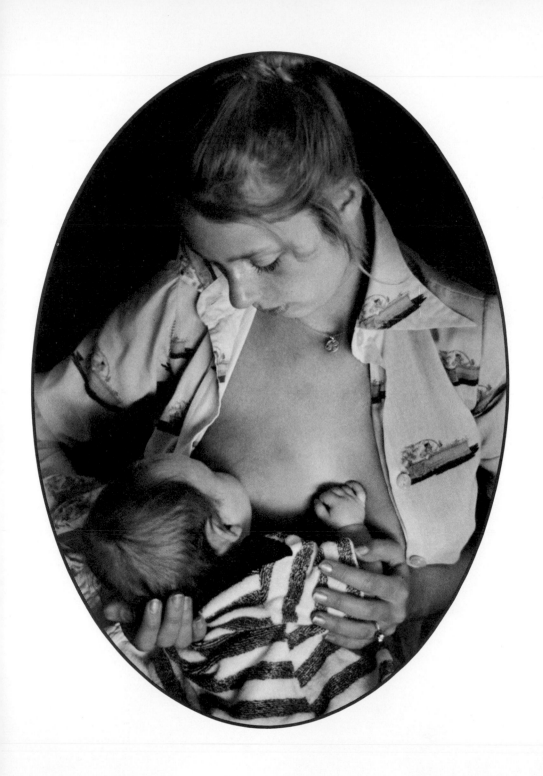

spring

Martin's endless night of heartbreak lifted soon after Virginia arrived as his teenage Belgian bride. She viewed her new life as the fulfilled reward of a dream. Even when he slipped and called her Dina—instantly mute with stunned chagrin—she would leap upon him, arms locked around his battered head, and then deluge him with kisses as though he had just presented her with the rarest jewel in the world.

When Barbara was born, to the often bemused elation of her mother, control of their home immediately fell into the already stubborn fists of a despot. She demanded absolute fealty of the bruised old street fighter. He was to surrender daily—a joyous prisoner in the wars she waged for his heart.

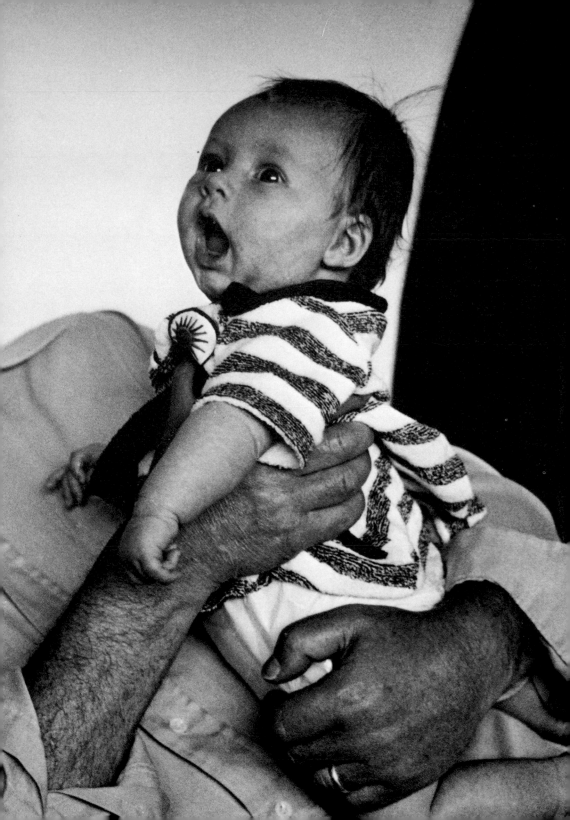

summer

Barbara was a child of nature. In summertime she probed for secrets in the garden that encircled the ancient farmhouse. Clutching the finger of her father, she leaned into the mistral's fury when exploring the edge of their ridge, where she could look out across the replanted mimosa forests of Tanneron. Each day of her second year overflowed with rich discoveries; old friends found little had changed in the eight years since the great fire. Plume grass and giant century plants bordered the fieldstone wall beside the old well with its beehive-shaped protective dome. It still gave enough water for flowers and the lawn, where Martin worked in the hot summer sun and shared his dreams with Virginia, while they awaited the arrival of Barbara's brother or sister, expected before Christmas. Martin's long night had ended.

Tanneron again became a sanctuary of hope and the source of new challenges for Martin. He once confessed that the most tortured night of his entire life was endured not while street fighting in the dark against Gestapo killers in the Warsaw ghetto, nor when mutilated in their prisons, where they crushed his hands and smashed his face, nor on facing Treblinka's horror, or even when Dina and all of his children died. It was the long night when Barbara was born. Then, he was flayed by the question of whether he had been marked, since his own birth, to endure continuing torment—and would that fate now be inherited by this newborn child? But not even Virginia beheld anything of that wounding inner battle, in which his willpower defeated yet another foe.

New lives and optimism dominated the hilltop where Virginia joyously carried another child. Martin spent many days altering the old house and replying to new readers of his book; multiple translations had blanketed the earth. Thousands of strangers sought his help, hoping that they might share a problem or their misery with a man who was sure to understand. No plea ever went unanswered.

They were shining days, filled with mystery and excitement for Barbara; an idyllic world. Darling paraded *her* wobbly new family across the lawn, then returned to deadly Samson— kept in nearby seclusion when visitors came in the daytime. He silently stalked shadows by night, tensed, protecting them all, when only Martin and he were awake . . . both expecting the unknown.

autumn

Another *vendange* was awaited throughout the land. And as lush grapes ripened in the vineyards, so did the fruit now rounding within Virginia. Barbara still shrilled with anticipation as each new day's treasure was unearthed, while shifts of Darling's pups clung as a warming cape around Virginia's knees when she ventured into their secret world, which was only the garden.

It was a peaceful, drowsy time of life for the young mother and her even younger new family. Tranquillity replenished itself, flowing with ever greater strength from its secret source within a man who might pass unnoticed on most city streets. Few traces of his past distinguished him from many other men who walk among us, every day.

Unless you could see through the scars to another world, hidden behind his face.

A man must create the world
of which he is the center.

The Martin Gray Family
would like to share with you
the joy of
Larissa
who arrived in our home
December Third at Tanneron

christmas

For My Family

*I wish you
the most impossible
of dreams . . .
may they sustain you
through each long night
and every troubled day
of your lives*

Martin

He was a man, take him for all in all,
I shall not look upon his like again.

HAMLET